DANIELLE REID

The Fabric of Love

ARPress
ILLUMINATING IDEAS
EMPOWERING VOICES

ARPress
45 Dan Road Suite 15
Canton MA 02021

Hotline: 1(800) 220-7660
Fax: 1(855) 752-6001

Ordering Information:
Quantity Sales. Special discounts are available on quantity purchases by corporations, associations, and others. For details, contact the publisher at the address above.

Printed in the United States of America.

ISBN-13   Paperback   979-8-89676-080-1
               eBook   979-8-89676-081-8

Library of Congress Control Number: 2019914670

CONTENTS

ACKNOWLEDGEMENTS

With love and gratitude to my husband and best friend, Ted, who understands and tolerates the 2:00 a.m. bursts of creative energy that compel me to be working at the computer instead of sleeping. Your encouragement and support are like a refreshing breeze.

Special thanks to my friend, Anne Ring, who is a creative sounding board for story ideas and an astute editor.

Carol Lucas has been a divine lightening rod for the creation of this collection. She prodded me during my moments of exasperation at complicated life experiences with her words of wisdom: "This too shall pass!" and "Instead of complaining, you should write a book about that." Many thanks to insightful volunteer readers Jennifer, Joni, Martha, and Millie whose kindness will be honored with eternal rewards.

With gratitude to Rev. Jim Angle for his obedience to the Lord's instructions and for his prayers.

With much appreciation to Dr. Grace Toney Edwards for inspiring and guiding new writers through the Annual Appalachian Summer Writers Conference in Radford, VA

PART 1

INTRODUCTION

THE AMAZING LOVE OF GOD

God does not demand a lot from us. All He asks us to do is believe in Him, trust in Him, worship Him, and tell others about Him. If we're really honest about it, we're more likely to share information about a good movie or restaurant than to share the amazing love of God.

I've been guilty of passing up precious opportunities to communicate the love of God to others; but recently, I've felt the need to push beyond my comfort zone. There are people in our own communities who are longing to know that God loves them; that He cares for them; that He understands the trials and hurts they are going through; and that He has a plan to help them.

While it is vital for everyone to hear about the love of God, people desperately need to see the awesome love of God in action! They need to see Christians loving each other as Jesus taught, and then sharing that love with them through our actions.

Writing this book is my immediate contribution to that effort. Disclosing these true-to-life stories is a huge step of faith for me because I am a person who highly values privacy. I hope people will see that conveying the awesome love of God is much more important than indulging our own self-interests.

May the stories in this book inspire you to step out of your comfort zone and find ways to share the love of God with those who need to see it in action.

THE FABRIC OF LOVE
By Danielle Reid

The frail woman struggled to carry the three bolts of wide cloth and plopped them down on the counter in front of the clerk. It was the delicate pastel colors that had immediately caught her attention, but when she ran the material through her fingers, it felt like liquid silk.

"What beautiful colors," the clerk commented as she unraveled the material from the first bolt. "How many yards do you want?" The woman reached in her pocket, fingering the pack of folded dollars that was to be her grocery and gas money for the week. "Ten yards of each, please," she responded.

The clerk measured the material, expertly pulling it off the tubular bolt in yard-long lengths. "Did you realize this is 60" wide?" she asked almost as a rhetorical question. Then, noticing the luxurious texture of the fabric, she commented "I don't remember seeing this fabric before, but it would make some lovely outfits for young girls. Is that what you're going to do with it?" It was the confirmation the woman had been looking for and a sweet smile swept across her face in acknowledgement. She frequented this fabric store, often finding unbelievable bargains and close-outs on upholstery materials; but today's shopping trip was different. It felt as if she was sent on a mission to purchase this specific cloth. She had wandered around the store, drinking in the rich colors and textures of the fabrics but not knowing exactly what she was looking for: until she saw the three bolts of material stuffed behind a seasonal display.

As the clerk finished measuring and calculating the purchase, she pulled a shopping cart from behind the counter and placed the cloth in the cart. "Do you need any thread or trim today?" she asked in the standard manner of upselling the customer.

Pausing for a moment to glance at the myriad of trim styles and colors, the woman reached in her pocket again briefly touching the folded dollars, then replied, "No thank you. This will be enough."

When she arrived at the check-out counter, she was grateful that the clerk had given her a shopping cart because the line was moving at a very slow pace. While this might irritate some people, it gave the frail woman an opportunity to chat with like-minded people. One gregarious woman ahead of her had several extra coupons and shared a 60% off-purchase-price coupon with her. The frail woman breathed a prayer, "Thank you, God! You truly supply our needs."

Although not a talented seamstress herself, the frail woman had a strong sense of style; coordinating colors and textures to create an image of elegance for her home. In years past, her income had allowed her to hire people to decorate and to create her wardrobe; but those days of luxury were gone, replaced by a meager fixed income.

It wasn't the downsizing that bothered her as much as the meager income; restricting her from extending an open hand to her favorite charities and individuals in need. She possessed a frail physical appearance, but inside this woman were deep waters of generosity and a strong desire to bless other people.

Placing her packages in the car, she arranged them as if they were a treasure to be protected, and then drove to the grocery store to purchase a few staple items that would sustain her during the week. When Wes, the grocery shelf stocker carried her bags to the car, she reached in her pocket and pulled out the last dollar bills. "College is starting soon. This may help with expenses," she said, placing it in his hands.

She drove home and parked her car in the garage that was nearly the same size as her tiny house. She carried her newly purchased treasure into the small spare bedroom that she used for storage. Placing the fabric on a shelf in the closet, she prayed that God would direct her in the use of it; and that it would be a blessing to the people who received it. She didn't know what God had planned or how he would bring His plan into existence, but she trusted Him to do it.

Many days passed without any apparent direction. The frail woman became involved with other projects and life issues; and the plans for the fabric seemed to be shelved, just as the actual fabric lay hidden on the shelf in the spare bedroom.

The church service that week was devoted to International Missions, and several groups of missionaries presented information about their ministries.

They touched the hearts of everyone with their stories of sacrifice and love while reaching the world with the Gospel.

After the service, the frail woman chatted with some of the missionaries and their families. One particular little girl named Jennie, whose parents had been missionaries for 12 years, captured the frail woman's heart. Although Jennie's parents were citizens of the richest nation in the world, they exchanged that right for a life of poverty and simplicity so they could live among the people who they were teaching and serving. She and her family had very few personal possessions and her clothes were hand-me-downs but that didn't appear to bother her. She was an extraordinarily happy little girl with a bright smile and a generous heart.

"This child has a destiny," the frail woman thought. Then a simple prayer passed through her lips and floated to the throne room of God, "Lord, while you were here on earth you loved and blessed the children. Show me what I can do to be a blessing to this child?"

Thoughts of Jennie and other missionary children preoccupied the frail woman throughout the following week. It was as if the frail woman was on her own mission to discover what she could do to bless them.

On Friday, a neighbor invited her to come over and meet his sister who was visiting for the weekend. He was trying to encourage his sister to buy a home and settle in the area. The frail woman baked a strawberry shortcake and presented it to the neighbor and his sister.

While they sat outside on the deck enjoying the shortcake, a rich cup of coffee and light conversation, God intervened. This wasn't merely a neighborly visit; it was a divinely orchestrated connection. As they chatted together, the sister began talking about her desire to restructure her life. She had managed a textile factory for 30 years and was looking for something else to do. Something with a purpose! Something that would bring joy to her heart!

It was if the frail woman felt the jolt of her Creator's divine connection; her eyes brightened as imagination started coalescing into a plan. She told the sister about buying the fabric and meeting the missionary children and how she wanted to bless them; but wasn't sure what the connection was…until now.

Sometimes the bonds of friendship are forged through adversity, but sometimes they are woven together thread by thread through a unified purpose.

The two women immediately began drawing on each other's experiences to develop a plan. The sister could purchase fabric directly from the textile mills. The frail woman had access to clothing patterns. And both ladies knew women who loved to sew — some of them were retired from the textile industry.

They began production with the goal of sewing one outfit for each female missionary child and sending it to her for Christmas. Soon, news of their efforts began to spread and others volunteered to help with the clothing project for the missionary children. The owner of a storage unit volunteered space to accumulate the packages until they were shipped. Sunday school groups collected money to help pay for the shipping. A fabric store donated thread and trim. Others volunteered to address the shipping labels.

Package upon package was wrapped in beautiful paper and tied with colorful ribbon. On each one was a card with the child's name, address and the name of the one who sewed the outfit. Volunteers came together to pray over the packages before they were shipped; and then everyone agreed to help with the project the following year.

Months passed and then a wonderful thing happened! The frail woman began receiving letters and cards addressed to "The Fabric of Love." They were from missionary children, their families and others explaining how they were blessed by receiving the beautiful outfits.

Tears of joy and gratitude flowed down her cheeks as she read each precious pronunciation of the Lord's love. One missionary child wrote that she never had a new dress of her own. Another child wrote that she felt the hug of God when she put on her new dress. A youngster wrote that she gave her new dress to a girl whose parents were pastors and had been persecuted because of their faith.

She shared the letters with the neighbor's sister and wondered how they had found her address. After all, she protested, many people volunteered and worked to bless these children.

The neighbor's sister smiled and confessed, "I had labels made and sewn into each dress. The labels said, 'Made by The Fabric of Love' and then a friend registered the company and established a non-profit organization in your name. You were the one through whom God chose to bless these children and inspire us. My dear friend, you wove us together as the fabric of love."

GABBY: THE PRO-LIFE LAMB

By Danielle Reid

I was having another one of those early morning conversations with the Lord – I had been awakened at 2:30 a.m. several times during the week. Now as I paced and prayed, I attempted to explain to God why I couldn't do what He asked me to do.

"My classmates will eat me alive," I exclaimed. "They think pro-life people are villains…that they all blow up buildings and shoot people, and that they're mean spirited…" I drifted off in my ramblings. But I couldn't shake the sense of obligation to tell my collage classmates about how much God loves them. I paced my living room for another hour praying for them individually.

At forty-eight, I had been given the opportunity through a private grant to return to college and complete my Bachelor's degree in Media Studies. I had two years to finish my degree and it really would be close, requiring me to take fifteen to eighteen credit hours per semester, including summer sessions.

My husband and I have grown children so the demands of a young family would not be a problem; but we own a working farm and were expanding into the cut flower business—which is labor-intensive. We agreed that although it would severely limit us financially, we would trust God to direct us, for we both felt my attaining this degree was something that the Lord had provided.

My Media and Society class was constructed to promote critical thinking skills and required us to write and have approved ten two-page position papers, including three interviews with people pertaining to the topic of the position paper; two oral class presentations; and three independent discussions with the professor.

During one of our class open discussions, the subject of abortion was brought up; and, as we all know, it is a very emotional topic. I sat and listened to my younger classmates venerate the reasons why abortion should be legal, unrestricted, private and unregulated. It was a litany of the typical reasons, coinciding with the Roe v. Wade 1972 Supreme Court decision.

Predictably, the discussion turned rather ugly as pro-life people were blamed for bombings, un-Christian like behavior, murdering abortionists, wanting to restrict a woman's constitutional rights, etc.

I tried to remain calm, but my emotions got the best of me. I deliberately asked a question: "Do you feel that the attitude of men has changed toward women since the passage of Roe v. Wade?" It was bantered about, and not directly responded to, so I asked it another way: "Do you think men are taking the responsibility for bringing new life into the world—or are they abandoning their responsibility to care for their child and the mother of their child?" We were out of class time, and as the question hung in the air, I felt that these college students were not using their critical thinking skills to address the issue. They were merely repeating the rhetoric that has been inculcated into our public education institutions and society.

Their characterization of my pro-life friends offended me; but then God gently reminded me that just a few years ago, I would have been in agreement with my fellow classmates, vehemently arguing on their side.

"Yes, I mused…you've come a long way baby!"

The classroom debate haunted me for several days and I discussed it with my husband and church friends. "We've got to reach them somehow! There must be a way to explain to them what it really means to be pro-life," I anguished.

My answer came during that 2:30 a.m. conversation with Jesus, the most pro-life person I've ever known. I acquiesced and started writing the position paper, knowing it would be my first oral class presentation.

On the day of the class presentation, a strange thing happened. I got confused with my class schedule. At 10:50 a.m., I realized that my class started at 11:00 a.m. and the campus was a twenty-five-minute drive from my home. Even though I rushed to get there, I was too late to give my oral presentation; it had to be rescheduled for another date. At first I was relieved and thought that maybe God just wanted me to be willing to present the prolife side of the issue. But that agonizing feeling rose within me again, knowing that these students needed to hear what God directed me to present to them. I immediately prayed for another opportunity to impart this information to my young classmates. My re-scheduled presentation date was Thursday, February 25th.

Tuesday, February 23

On Tuesday, February 23rd, our sheep started lambing and from the start, I could tell that this wasn't going to be a normal lambing process. My husband had scheduled appointments and had to leave the farm early in the morning; but I revisited the barn several times hoping the ewe would handle the process on her own. By 10:00 a.m. I realized the birthing ewe was in distress.

When my husband called for a progress report, I encouraged him to come home.

The lamb was in a breach-birth position and had to be turned before being gently pulled from the mother's womb. It takes one person to hold and steady the ewe and the other to perform the birthing functions, so we worked together as if we were a skilled surgical team. After the lamb was born, the mother still seemed agitated and we believed she would have twins. We waited thirty-minutes, but nothing happened. By now I had missed my Media and Society class and decided to stay and help my husband with the ewe.

(The penalty for missing more than two classes is dropping a letter grade, and I had worked very hard to maintain a high grade-point average.) Another hour went by and we decided we needed to probe for another lamb, possibly lodged in the birth canal. The ewe was not in agreement! We did discover another lamb that needed to be turned, and the second lamb was born. By now, the first lamb, which we named Gabby, was beginning to get weak. The ewe's milk was not flowing, so we warmed and fed Gabby some frozen colostrum that we keep on hand for emergencies.

While we were at the house retrieving and warming the colostrum, the ewe birthed a third lamb. Even though she was exhausted, the ewe was trying to clean and nurture the second two lambs, which were much more energetic than little Gabby. The ewe called to each lamb in a low tone, and they chorused back with their muted little "baaa's." But Gabby was too weak and confused to reply.

We continually checked on the lambs' progress every hour. Several hours later, the two lambs were beginning to bounce around the lambing pen, recuperating rapidly from their birth trauma; but little Gabby remained very weak. She would try to nurse from her mother, but the ewe would walk away from Gabby's feeble nursing attempts; while her two boisterous brother lambs pushed her even farther away from the ewe.

Whenever we would visit the lambing pen we would pray for Gabby and ask God to strengthen and sustain her during this difficult period of her delicate life. Then we would go through the frustrating function of trying to milk the ewe or to get her to stand still so Gabby could nurse.

Most people in our society have never experienced living on a working farm; and don't understand the life and death struggle being played out before our eyes. We have seen innocent little lambs perish even when we have done everything in our power to keep them alive. For Gabby, we searched through the lambing books and called more experienced people who are familiar with this kind of dilemma, seeking answers; but we rejected most of the advice we received.

Thursday, February 25

Two days later, before dawn, the ewe in the adjacent lambing pen gave birth to a very large single lamb; but when we made our barn check that morning, the single lamb was dead. The ewe was frantically pacing in her pen, crying and pawing the dead baby, as if trying to make it stand up. It appeared to be a tragedy for her and for us… but God can use what seems bad and turn it into something positive.

(Of course, this was my Media and Society class day, and if I missed this class the penalty was to drop a letter grade.)

We realized that this tragedy could be Gabby's only window of opportunity to live, so my husband and I had to move quickly to accomplish our goal. In rare occasions, if you are persistent, you can "graft" a lamb onto a ewe that has lost her baby. It takes monumental effort, but we felt it was the only solution for weak little Gabby, who by now was being ignored by her mother and stepped on by her healthy, larger brothers.

There are several ways to entice a ewe to accept a lamb that is not hers— one that requires removing the hide of the dead lamb and wrapping it around the live one; but we didn't have the fortitude to attempt that strategy. Instead, we rubbed the dead lamb all over Gabby trying to transfer the birth scent onto her, and presented Gabby to the frantic ewe. You can imagine the chaos in the lambing pen with a frenzied mother, a feeble and confused lamb, and us trying to challenge the course of nature. "Lord, just this one time," I prayed.

Our attempts to hold the ewe steady and place Gabby at the ewe's nipple, giving her much-needed nourishment, failed miserably. Gabby was too confused and feeble to nurse for herself and the ewe didn't appreciate our intrusion. The ewe kicked and out maneuvered us, and the frustration level in all of us reached the boiling point.

"Why can't you just settle down and adopt this baby!" I yelled at the ewe.

"She needs you—you're her only chance!" We took time out to pray, and then hit upon a strategy that would work. While lambs nurse, they snuggle up to their mothers with their heads tucked under her belly, their sides touching hers, and their tails facing their mother's head. The mother then encourages the lamb to nurse by licking its tail area and "talking" to it. We reasoned that if we could get the surrogate ewe's milk into Gabby, the ewe would think it was her lamb; and accept it as it stood in the natural nursing position.

It was an unpleasant session, but we wrestled the ewe down, and got enough sheep milk for several feedings. Then the next problem was trying to feed Gabby without her imprinting on us instead of the ewe. We decided that we would leave Gabby in the pen with the surrogate mother and every few hours, take a bottle of the surrogate ewe's milk to the lambing pen. We would then securely tie a lead line to the ewe's halter and on our hands and knees, prop Gabby up against the ewe in the nursing position, and slide the bottle into Gabby's mouth from the opposite side of the ewe. That way, Gabby would think that she was nursing from the ewe and the ewe would get used to Gabby. Eventually this strategy worked!

I didn't have time to take a shower before leaving for my Media and Society class and I probably smelled like wet wool, after the wrestling match with the surrogate ewe. I was a few minutes late for class and asked the professor's and class forgiveness for the interruption, after explaining about the lambing problems we were having. The students seemed quite interested in the sweet little lambs and asked several questions before settling into another intense debate. Fortunately, we ran out of class time before my presentation and it was rescheduled again.

Miraculously, the ewe accepted Gabby and for the next few days all was well at the lambing pens; but God had a bigger plan for Gabby, and it was about to unfold in the college classroom.

As I argued with God during that early-morning prayer time on Saturday, He revealed the presentation He wanted me to give on Tuesday, my next class. I was to take Gabby with me, and use the lamb as a living prop in my oral presentation.

Tuesday, March 2

On Tuesday, I was up early and praying...a lot...about the class presentation. I didn't take the prepared script with me because I felt assured that God would give me the words to say and how to say them. This would not be a polished, rehearsed presentation; more like a humble shepherd, speaking straight from the heart.

Because Gabby had been hugged and handled from birth, she was not afraid of me and was completely docile during the twenty-five minute drive; and so quiet in the classroom that the professor did not realize I had a live lamb until I stood in front of the class to deliver my speech.

I held Gabby in my arms and slowly paced in front of the spellbound students, explaining that she was why I had been late for class the previous week. Everyone melted at the sight of this innocent, helpless life and when she softly baaaa-ed, they "ooh-ed" and "aaah-ed" in response. God had them right where He wanted them.

I explained about the problems we had with birthing triplet lambs, how Gabby had gotten weak, and was rejected by her mother. I talked about the process we used to try to save Gabby; and about the phone calls we had made seeking the expertise of more knowledgeable people.

"The first person we called said he had tried to pull these orphan lambs through several times... but it wasn't worth the time and aggravation. His solution was to just leave the lamb in the pen with the mother, ignore its cries, and in a few days... it would die. Your problem would be solved," he reasoned.

The facial expressions of the students changed as they thought of how hard-hearted someone had to be to ignore the cries of this newborn lamb, nestled in my protective embrace.

"The next person we called said he'd fill a tub with water, plunge the lamb into the tub, and hold its head under water until it drowned—like you would an unwanted litter of puppies."

Groans emitted from the students as they gazed upon innocent little Gabby, so content in my arms.

"Since we didn't like either of those suggestions, we made another call.

We were told that these orphans never amount to much. "What you need to do is get it over quick. Pick up the lamb by the head and snap its neck real quick. It's over and done with and you don't have any more worries," was the last caller's plan.

By now, some students had their heads down on their desks, moaning, as others' fought back tears.

Then I stopped my pacing, re-adjusted Gabby in my arms and calmly stated, "Today, we're going to talk about what it means to be pro-life…" As if on cue, Gabby lifted her little face and softly bleated, "b-a-a-a." I explained to my younger classmates how I used to agree with many of them that abortion was a woman's choice…that is… until I had a personal encounter at age 40 with Jesus Christ; and finally understood what pro-life really means. I was able to tell them about the unconditional love that God has for them; that there is forgiveness and healing for them if they had participated in an abortion; and how true Christians love them and pray for them.

I don't know the long-term impact that speech had, but God knows. Often, God uses word-pictures to capture the heart of the issue better than arguments.

Interestingly, this was a Spiritual turning point for me. I learned that when God asks you to step out of your comfort zone and do something for Him, you don't have to be afraid. Just be willing. He will supply the Lamb!

WHEN WE BETRAY GOD
By Danielle Reid

I wasn't sure if it was the thunder clap rattling the open windows or the strobe light effects of the lightning that shattered my sleep. The result was the same: a flood of fear swept over me. I considered gathering the dogs and heading for the basement but the thought of retreating to a cold, musty cellar kept me immobile in a more comfortable place. Eventually, the clamor of the storm grew dim as it moved beyond the boundaries of our valley. I breathed a prayer of thanks that the builders of our 150-year-old-log home had been diligent in constructing it.

Where this storm came from was a mystery to me. I had checked the forecast before retiring for the night and had heard no warnings on the weather channel or radio.

I had just dozed off again when the phone rang. It was after midnight. The voice on the other end of the phone was sobbing making it impossible for me to understand the dilemma.

"Slow down," I pleaded. "I can't understand you. And if I can't understand you, I can't help you. Take three deep breaths," I suggested.

My friend Sandy regained her composure and began to explain the reason for her frantic phone call.

"I'm so sorry to call you this late, but I had to talk with you," she sobbed.

We'd known each other since we were toddlers and had a rapport that equaled our closest family members.

"Have you ever felt betrayed?" she asked. "I can't believe it, but I feel like Bill has… betrayed me."

Bill was her husband of 40 years-a strong man in character and physique, and a diligent worker. Years ago, he began a business out of their garage which had become a successful company, employing several full-time workers.

"What do you mean, Sandy? Bill wouldn't cheat on ...." My conversation was interrupted before I could complete the sentence.

"No! No! Not that kind of betrayal," she said. "Let me tell you what just happened. Bill has been sort of ...you know...grouchy lately... kind of short tempered, which is not like him. He's been spending more time in his office, and I thought something was strange; but I've also been busy with my job, so I dismissed it."

Sandy had worked for a well established company as an administrator for 20 years. She was planning to retire in a few months with goals of spending time with their grandchildren and becoming more involved in volunteerism and community service.

"While I was at work this afternoon, we were interrupted by auditors and given 1-hour to clean out our offices and leave because the company assets had been seized, and the company was in bankruptcy. You know what this means? No retirement. The first thing to get cut is the retirees' benefits. All my time and money invested in this company is wasted. I'm 63-years-old. There is no way I can work long enough at another company to earn retirement benefits." By now, Sandy was sobbing again.

After regaining her composure she continued, "But, that's not the worst part. It was after 5:00pm when I got to Bill's office to tell him what happened, and I heard him talking on the phone. As I waited in the hallway, I heard him pleading with someone to give him more time to pay them. I was shocked. I thought Bill's company was doing well."

"I left his office and drove around for awhile trying to sort out the day's events. I decided to give Bill the opportunity of talking with me about it before confronting him, so I drove home and prepared his favorite dinner.

You know, Southern comfort food has soothed many arguments." "All evening, I dropped hints and asked leading questions, but by 9:00pm, Bill hadn't confided in me about his business problems. Then I disclosed what I heard and asked what was going on."

"Bill tried to explain how sales had plummeted because of overseas competition and that he owed money to several of his suppliers – huge amounts that he couldn't pay back without increased sales. He'd been spending extra time at the office trying to develop new customers, but with fears about the instability of the economy, businesses weren't expanding or investing in inventory."

"'We're through,'" he confessed to me. "'I can't see any way out of this except to close the company and sell off the assets to pay my creditors. We may have to sell the house, too.'"

"I was numb and blurted out, 'But why didn't you tell me this before? Why were you hiding this from me?'"

Sandy was crying again and I could feel her intense emotional pain as she said that Bill kept the news from her to protect her. "But what he didn't understand is that now I feel betrayed, because he didn't trust me!" I suggested that we both take a moment to allow our emotions to calm down.

Sandy was the first to speak. "I felt like the world was crushing me and I couldn't breathe."

"I lay on the bedroom floor curled up in a fetal position, cowering under my bed; my only awareness was my own voice hoarsely whispering repeatedly, 'I'm the head and not the tail. I'm a child of God and a co-laborer with Christ...'"

"I had no energy and felt confused; but deep inside, beyond the realm of conscious thought, a tiny bit of knowledge made its way into my memory.

Fragments of scripture verses that I had read or memorized began to filter through my mind. I remembered what King David did after the devastating attack at Ziklag. Instead of cursing God, he encouraged himself in the Lord (I Samuel 30:1-6). More scripture verses began to flood in: Moses' understudy, Joshua, was instructed by God not to fear but to speak the Word as he went about his daily duties (Joshua 1:8-9). Still more verses: The people of Israel were instructed by God to send the praise and worship leaders ahead of the army into battle; and their army would be victorious."

"I endured two-and-a-half hours of this mental battle before I was able to get off the floor and crawl into bed – still exhausted and still whispering scripture verses. Then I called you."

After praying together and agreeing to talk the next day, we ended our midnight conversation.

My sleep was intermittent and restless.

For days I wondered about this incident. Was the victory that Sandy survived the emotional storm with her mental faculties in place; or was there something more? What was the significance and what was she supposed to do with it?

A heart-heaviness set in. It wasn't depression, but more like a wound left unattended. Then during a session of restless sleep one night, the realization came to me. Sandy had not only felt betrayed by her husband, but she also felt betrayed and abandoned by God.

I breached my own comfort zone and began to talk with other Christian friends and discovered that many of them were enduring hardships and testing of their faith, beyond anything they had experienced in the past. They were good people so why was life so difficult now?

Didn't the Bible say that the righteous would prosper? But every financial endeavor that had worked in the past was now failing.

Income steams had drastically dropped off and Sandy was unemployed, even though she had a college degree.

Didn't the Bible illustrate the Body of Christ meeting together and having fellowship? But Sandy felt like a step-child and rarely received calls from her church family when she needed them the most.

Didn't the Bible state that healing and wholeness belonged to the believer?

But there had been an auto accident a few years ago that wasn't her fault, and left her in constant pain.

Didn't I read in the Bible that our flocks and herds (pets) would multiply and prosper? But a careless neighbor's dogs had attacked and killed two registered dogs Sandy used for breeding.

Nothing was making sense! Sandy and my Christian friends were experiencing pain, separation, rejection, and unfulfilled expectations, all brought on by others. Some began to question their salvation. If the message of the Bible was true, then why was all this terrible stuff happening?

Sandy's experience forced me to look deeper into myself and my relationship with God. I still didn't understand what was happening… so in desperation I ran the Christian-ese checklist

- tithe
- attend church services
- pray
- read the Bible
- give to missions and ministries.

Although I was attending Sunday church services, there were mid-week services that I frequently missed. My tithing was ok, but maybe I wasn't giving as much to worthy causes as I used to – and instead, spending more money on family entertainment. My prayer life? Well, those early morning intercessory prayer sessions that I used to love had transformed into a few minutes of prayer while driving to work. And when was the last time that I really studied the Bible? I couldn't speak for anyone else, but my spiritual life needed some serious CPR!

Sandy and I had several more conversations which resulted in changing our focus from self to Him. The Bible tells us that Jesus was tested in all points of His humanity…just like we are. He knows and understands separation, pain, rejection, false accusations, and expectation.

Yet during those excruciating trials and torture, Jesus didn't betray His father or His purpose. How could He stand against all hell breaking over Him and not be fearful or angry?

Then it occurred to me: the opposite of love is fear, not hate. Our negative emotions are based in fear. Think about it: fear of rejection, fear of loss, fear of failure, fear of death.

But God's Word is full of Love beginning with the Old Testament and continuing throughout the New Testament. It declares that God is the very essence of Love.

I John 4:7-18 tells us a lot about love. Here is what verse 18 states: "There is no fear in love. But perfect love drives out fear, because fear has to do with punishment."

That last phrase of the sentence was a key to unlocking Sandy's dark emotional state. By living in fear, was she betraying the very essence of God; and expecting an angry and disappointed god to punish her for her humanity?

In I Corinthians 13, we are reminded that Love always protects, Love always trusts, Love always hopes, Love always perseveres, Love never fails.

As Christians, can we display those characteristics of Love while living in fear? Can we proclaim that we are wholeheartedly trusting God? Have we betrayed Him by not completely embracing His greatest commandment: Love?

Fortunately, like the prodigal son's father who daily searched the road leading to his house, God searches our hearts and calls us back to Him. His remedy for our betrayal is to Love us back into His kingdom. What an amazing God!

I had some decisions to make that would compel me to move beyond my comfort zone. So did Sandy and Bill. As time progressed, they realized that they needed to put their faith into practice. They began by making daily prayer a top priority. Eventually, they added fasting one day a week; and volunteering at their church's food bank.

Sandy's trial helped me realize that there are areas of my life that need correction and improvement, but I no longer have to be afraid to face that reality because the fear of punishment is gone. And although we are responsible for our choices, and there are consequences for our actions, I know that God loves us with an unending love – much deeper, much richer, much stronger than we can imagine! He will never betray us and as long as we abide in Love, as Jesus commanded, then we will not betray Him.

POEMS

THE WISDOM OF GOD

How did You hang the sun and moon
and what keeps the stars in place?

What are galaxies made of
and how vast is outer space?

How did You teach the ocean waves
to gently kiss the shore?

Did You raise the mountains up so high
they could knock on Heaven's door?

How does each seed and blade of grass
spring forth from under the earth?

Do songbirds that cruise the azure sky
know what their melody is worth?

When You formed mankind from the ancient dust
and breathed life into his soul

Had You already planned that Your Righteous Son
would come to make us whole?

THE HOLY SPIRIT DWELLS IN ME

By Danielle Reid

He whispers to me and my heart responds
*   from the depth of my spirit*
*   deep calls to deep*
*   Spirit to spirit*
*   life giving dynamos*
*   bringing newness and strength*

He sends knowledge on the wings of His Truth
*   and my understanding grows*
*   eternal wisdom*
*   unspeakable glory*
*   of things to come*

My love for Him overflows
*   as I remember His gift of sacrifice*
*   unconditional Love*
*   forgiveness*
*   restoration*

My heart feels like fire
*   when He sends the Refiner*
*   white hot conviction*
*   consuming my transgressions*
*   for growth and guidance*
*   training and preparation*

Tears flow in repentance
    and temper the Refiner's fire
        I'm not ashamed of my love for Him
        He is my strength
        my world
        my life
        my friend forever
        both here and hereafter

*   This was a ten-minute writing assignment using the theme "_____ dwells in me" during the Appalachian Summer Writer's Conference

I WILL SING IN THE SHADOW OF YOUR WINGS

I will sing in the shadow of your wings
Lord Jesus
I will sing in the shadow of your wings

I will dance with joy
And shout your praises
I will sing in the shadow of your wings

In the shadow of your wings
My needs are met
In the shadow of your wings
There's no regret
In the shadow of your wings
My life is blessed
I will sing in the shadow of your wings

I will sing in the shadow of your wings
Lord Jesus
I will sing in the shadow of your wings

I will clap my hands
And shout your praises
I will sing in the shadow of your wings

In the shadow of your wings
I find great peace
In the shadow of your wings
There's sweet release
In the shadow of your wings
My life's complete
I will sing in the shadow of your wings

*　This was inspired while going through a difficult season of life, and came in
the form of a song.

PART II

INTRODUCTION

ARISE MY LOVE

Isaiah 43: 18-19 Forget the former things; do not dwell on the past. See I am doing a new thing! Now it springs forth; do you not perceive it? I am making a way in the desert and streams in the wasteland.

Do you know anyone who is a late bloomer? A late bloomer is a person who does not discover his/her talents and abilities until later in life than normally expected. There is a common belief that intellectual development hits the highest point in a young adult and then slowly declines with age. However, this perception does not recognize that the older person has the advantage of accumulated knowledge, associations between concepts and mental techniques.

Here are some late bloomers you may recognize:

Danny Aiello and Rodney Dangerfield did not begin acting until they were in their 40s.

Grandma Moses began her painting career in her 70s.

Harland David "Colonel" Sanders began his Kentucky Fried Chicken franchise in his 60s.

Marjory Stoneman Douglas founded "Friends of the Everglades" when she was 78.

Laura Ingalls Wilder published her first novel, "Little House on the Prairie," in her 60s.

While searching the internet for the subject of late-bloomers, I found blogs from individuals in their 30s and 40s who were panicking because they hadn't achieved what they consider success. I used to be one of those stressed-out late-bloomers but I learned to forget the past failures, hurts and disappointments—and trust God. That is when He brought His streams of refreshing into my life…and proclaimed, "Arise my love!" Although I saw myself through negative eyes, God saw me through the eyes of the Creator. He knew the plan He had for my life and brought it forth, despite my trying to run, hide and refuse His love.

I hope these stories inspire you to seek God's carefully designed plan for your life. Abraham and Sarah did, and look what they accomplished as late bloomers.

LATE BLOOMERS

Historical biographies trace the lives of the world's most influential and prestigious people. Some of these famous people had tenuous starts in life but managed to overcome their fragile beginnings and leave enduring legacies.

Thomas Edison flunked elementary math, and had it not been for his astute mother who tutored him at home, he might have been written off as a loser.

Later in life, Edison discovered how to harness electricity and enlightened the world. Sir Isaac Newton was born during a great famine to a destitute widow.

He wasn't expected to live through the next day but she begged neighbors to pray for him. Later in his life, Newton developed theories that would change the study of science and math. Not many people know that he used those math skills to unlock Biblical secrets and ancient mathematical calculations.

But what about the rest of us over 40, who haven't yet left indelible footprints in the sands of time and whose names probably will not appear in future editions of Who's Who? Can our lives have significance as late bloomers?

There are numerous reasons why people become late-bloomers. Like Newton, you might have had a difficult start in life. Maybe you were abandoned, or from a family experiencing poverty, or living in a society undergoing social or political upheaval. Maybe there was an accident and you had to learn basic life skills all over again. Or maybe you made it through childhood unscathed, but something in your adult life caused you to be derailed.

Sometimes it seems as if life acts like a bully—screaming in your face and pushing you down every time you try to get back on your feet.

My childhood wasn't perfect and I reacted to events in negative ways. I took everything personally and internalized all the failures. Because of some of the struggles and ordeals, I retreated emotionally, became cynical and didn't trust people.

When life is out of balance, it is much more difficult to achieve personal goals and relate well to others. It took me to age 40 before I got a handle on how to improve personal relationships; age 50 before I received my undergraduate college degree; age 55 before writing a children's book series; and to age 60 before I earned my M.S. Education degree.

Although the educational achievements are wonderful, my most important life lesson had to do with relationship. We were living in South Carolina at that time, restoring a 100-year-old country home which we recently purchased for our retirement residence. During the renovation process, something strange happened and I became ill. In a matter of three days, I felt like I was going to die. I was desperate. As I lay on the couch in our darkened apartment, depressed and afraid, a Christian program came on the TV. The speaker's words reached out to me and I summoned the courage to call the prayer line for help.

Living in America where there are numerous churches in every community, you'd think that I would have heard the phrase, "You must be born again." Oh, I attended Sunday school as a child and church as a teenager because I had a crush on the pastor's son; but in my 40 years of life, I didn't recall hearing the phrase about being born again.

The Christian prayer counselor patiently explained what it meant to be born again; and I opened my heart to the gift of unconditional Love that Jesus Christ offered through His sacrifice. It seemed as if a heavy burden was lifted off of me and I no longer felt fearful.

It's important to emphasize that accepting Jesus Christ as your Savior is not the final step; rather, it is the first step in an eternal relationship that will continue to improve if you are willing to invest your time and your effort.

I confided in a friend living in our apartment complex what I had done. She was happy for me and invited me to her church down the street. She explained about the church's great softball team and the fun she had during ladies-night-out events. I was excited.

But, a funny thing happened on the way to the church. I assumed my friend's church was the only one on the block and stopped at the first church I came to. I looked for her several times during services, but never saw her.

That's because this wasn't her church. This church was unlike any I had ever been in. There was amazing music and people stood up to honor and praise God. Every time I attended the services, I would cry; so I sat in the back row close to the door—in case it got too intense, I could leave without disturbing anyone. One Sunday, two elderly ladies asked me to sit with them and I agreed—not knowing their seats were in the center first row. They hemmed me in on both sides! Well, that morning there was intense prayer and praise. Someone prayed for me and it felt like warm liquid love was flowing all over me.

After that event, I started waking up at 2:00 a.m. with an unquenchable desire to study my Bible and pray. It was as if I had been assigned a personal trainer to guide me through the Bible (God's Word) and help me understand this new relationship with my Heavenly Father.

There was a cleansing process going on, too. Up until this time I had been filled with fear, anger, long-term grudges and self-contempt. I avoided mirrors and refused to have my picture taken. But as I yielded to this new relationship with my Heavenly Father, my personal relationships began to improve.

By now, we had moved into our partially renovated home and were intensely continuing the remodeling process—much like the spiritual renovation that the Lord was taking me through.

During one 2:00 a.m. prayer session, I was in the kitchen reading my Bible and searching for answers to a key question many of us have...why do bad things happen to good people?

"If you are such a good God, why did all those terrible things happen to me when I was a child? Where were you when I fell through the ice and almost drowned?"

The incident I was referring to happened when I was about seven years old. We lived a short distance from the shore of Lake Erie. One spring day, some of us decided to hike down Devil's Backbone—a steep cliff overlooking the lake. This place was never sanctioned by our parents and if they'd known about it, we would have been grounded.

We slipped and slid down the steep cliff and played on the lake shore for awhile. Then one of the group members yelled, "Let's claim ice castles!" and raced out onto the ice. Ice castles form as the waves crash and the wind freezes them in mid-air. We were about 200 yards off shore where the water is probably 20 feet deep. Several of us saw the biggest ice castle of them all and raced to claim it. My sister ran to the left, but I ran straight toward it... and fell through the ice into the frigid water.

My snow suit and boots immediately became waterlogged and dragged me down. I remember hearing the water close over my head and saw my air bubbles rising to the surface. I swam upward and surfaced long enough to gasp for air and hear my sister screaming. One of the dangers of falling through the ice is being swept under it by the current; but amazingly, I surfaced two more times at the same spot and grappled to get out, but the ice kept breaking in front of me. Someone grabbed a stick but poked me in the face with it, instead of helping me.

The next thing I remember is shivering while sitting at a campfire my sister had started. Someone had given me their coat and hat, and someone else their boots. We were afraid that our parents would find out and punish us, so the plan was to get my clothes dry before going home. Apparently, a family living on the cliff saw the campfire and came to investigate. They gave us a ride home and made us explain to our parents what happened. My mother hugged us and cried for a long time.

Anger rose up in my heart as I thought about the near drowning and I shouted the question again, "Where were you God when I almost drowned?"

You know, God doesn't react to our negative emotions. Instead, He may ask us a question in response. In my heart, I heard His question, "Do you remember the hands on your hips when you were struggling in the water?"

Immediately in a flash back, I could feel two strong hands resting on my hips, pushing me upward. "What are you telling me? That You were there rescuing me from drowning?" As the realization hit, I fell to my knees and sobbed uncontrollably. Later that day, I called my sister and asked her to describe the incident and explain how I got out of the water. She stated that it was almost as if I burst out of the water like a seal and rolled onto the ice away from the place I had fallen through!

There were several more intense sessions like this one. One time, hurtful events and words spoken against me from my past were placed on what appeared to be video tapes; then I flung them toward the sun (Son?) and watched them disintegrate. I felt compelled to call people whom I had hurt and ask their forgiveness. I experienced great joy that day as I forgave everyone who had hurt me and received forgiveness from others I had offended.

For 40 years I had doubts that God cared about what happened to each of us. Now, here was the proof, provided in a way I could understand and accept.

Maybe you've had similar experiences. Maybe those close to you—who should have been there to encourage and protect you—abandoned you instead. Holding grudges against them only hurts and immobilizes you. Right now, you can choose to allow God to bring healing and joy into your life.

As a late bloomer, I may never achieve greatness the way society defines it – but that's no longer important to me. What I have discovered is that God can impact anyone's life, at any stage of life, if they are willing to establish a personal relationship with Him.

Forget the hurts, disappointments and failures of the past. Forgive the people who hurt you and ask forgiveness from those you hurt. Then move forward and allow God to do a new thing in your life. He will nurture and strengthen you as He brings forth His plans and establishes His path for you to follow.

THE NEIGHBORHOOD

Family business brought me back to the hometown of my youth. My family had been proud Westsiders: hardworking, middle class, flag-waving Americans…at least since 1910 when my grandparents joined the great emigration through Ellis Island.

I was compelled to return to the neighborhood—my haven during my formative years. I still remember the address rehearsed on the first day of kindergarten: 434 Shenley Drive. Somehow, the houses looked smaller and closer together now. The towering elm trees whose giant limbs bowed over the boulevard and sheltered my older sister and me while we played were gone, replaced with tiny Bradford pear trees.

Back then, we knew all of our neighbors and talked to each other as we went about our daily chores. The adults watched over each other's kids and knew which ones belonged in the neighborhood. If one of us kids got in trouble, we could be assured that we were "gonna' get it" when our own Father got home.

I can envision the old neighborhood and hear the familiar street noises drifting through the perpetually unlocked screen doors. Natucci's lived in the two-story brick house on the corner. Patty was my best friend and confidant of childhood secrets. Stephanelli's had seven kids and occupied the grey house on the opposite side of the street – the one with the large front porch where Mama Rosa would dispatch them when they became too rowdy.

Torrelino's lived next door and had three good looking sons. In the middle of the block lived our most distinguished family: nurse and doctor, who made themselves available off hours to anyone in the neighborhood. We always wondered why Dr. Pearson didn't have a name ending in "i" or "o"; but he and his family were accepted anyway.

As I stood there on the boulevard, a flood of memories washed over me. A few good memories—but they were overpowered by other memories: the heart-wrenching ones, when I was torn from my utopia and flung into an insecure world my tender heart wasn't willing to accept.

I remember the incident when my life changed. I was about four years old. There was loud arguing, a door slamming…then bleak silence. That door slam became a recurring nightmare that I would endure until I was 40 years old. I would wake up panicked in a cold sweat, feeling the reverberation of that door slamming shut; and hearing the steel lock click in front of my face.

In my childhood inexperience, I couldn't understand the intricacies of adult human relationships, so I turned the feelings of confusion inward. It must have been something I said or did that caused my Daddy to be angry. Maybe if I was smarter, or more obedient, or prettier…maybe then my Daddy would still be living with us.

My Mother and Grandmother struggled to keep up appearances, but when their savings ran out, they accepted help from their family. Although my Daddy paid child support, eventually my Mother was forced to go to work.

She made $32.00 a week as a receptionist and her meager income was not adequate to care for us. My beautiful, talented, adoring Mother was no longer there to greet us when we came home from school. She no longer had the time or energy to sit on the front porch with admiring youngsters from the neighborhood at her feet while she captured our imaginations with her stories and freehand pastel drawings.

Eventually my Daddy made a trip to Reno to divorce my Mother; then onto Mexico City for a honeymoon with his new younger wife. My Mother's family was enraged and a battle for my sister's and my affections began between the families.

Our lives were now regimented by a legal schedule. On the weekends, my sister and I were shuttled to my father's fashionable house where our new step-mother lived. She had a daughter from a previous marriage and in my imagination, her daughter took my place in my father's life. The weekend transitions traumatized me and caused emotional upheavals. The guilt I was feeling pushed me further away from the people who loved me. I was becoming an angry and rebellious child.

During the weekdays in my Mother's absence, my elderly Grandmother was our guardian. Almost as a daily ritual, she would toast cheese sandwiches in a cast-iron frying pan and serve them on colorful Fiesta plates at the kitchen's white ceramic table. Then she would lie down for an afternoon nap. Sometimes my sister and I would have to turn off the gas stove burners before joining her.

One spring afternoon, I returned home for lunch. My older sister and I had been playing at the Pearson's house for most of the morning. I couldn't find my Grandmother and searched all through the house, calling to her. I discovered her lying on the tiled bathroom floor, barely conscious; but able to mumble that she couldn't get up. My six-year-old body was not capable of lifting her, even though I tried several times to hoist her to her knees. I ran back to my sister and her friends at the Pearson's. They only laughed and wouldn't believe that my precious Grandmother needed help! Several times I frantically ran back and forth between my house and the Pearson's, stumbling over the boulevard curb, and badly scraping my hands and knees. I was screaming for help when Mrs. Pearson heard my frantic cries and came to the rescue.

My Grandmother died that night. I remember my Mother hugging us and rocking back and forth, huddled together on her bed, as she tearfully repeated the essential details. I don't remember anything about the funeral...or much of my childhood after that.

Without my Grandmother's social security check, we couldn't afford to stay in the neighborhood. We relocated to an inner city apartment where noisy traffic and car headlights flashed through my bedroom at night, interrupting my sleep. Anger and tears were my constant companions.

I retreated into a dark realm of self-pity, always questioning my abilities and seeing myself as shameful and weak. I felt responsible for the family's loss. As I grew older, I continuously rehearsed the "if only…" scenarios and questioned my effectiveness in almost every situation.

The weight of that reality haunted my life until a few weeks ago, when I was talking about the incident with my sister. I recalled how guilty I felt all these years; and wondered how our lives would have been different if our Grandmother hadn't died that night.

To my surprise my sister responded, "Why should you feel guilty? I was the one who was responsible."

"Why do you say that?" I asked.

"Don't you remember the day that it happened?"

"I just told you I did. I remember everything about that terrible day," I retorted.

"No! Don't you remember what Day it was when that happened," she pursued.

"Tell me, because you're the one who can recall details about our childhood, like what color the wallpaper was in our bedroom." My voice was raising at least an octave and was bordering on shrill. This was a very touchy subject for me.

"It was April 1st…April Fool's Day! I thought you made up the story about Grandma because you were jealous that Cindy Pearson and I wouldn't let you play with us," she confessed.

The moment was suspended in stunned silence. All these years—50 of them—I had carried the burden of guilt…that because I was powerless and incompetent, I had killed my Grandmother and destroyed our family's future!

Now I was free of that burden! In one instant, I saw the lie for what it was and put it to death. I could return to my childhood memories, unafraid to face the past and released from the guilt that haunted me for my entire life!

Since that conversation with my sister, I've been able to reflect on many of the good childhood experiences. She has helped me remember funny anecdotes and other childhood adventures I had blocked out of my life.

That's why I felt compelled to return to the neighborhood. My visit would serve as closure to the years of pain.

Tears splattered on the inside of my eye glasses as I stood on the grassy boulevard in front of 434 Shenley Drive. The neighborhood had changed— and I had moved on.

No one approached me, asking who I was and what business I had there. I was a stranger to them—but no longer a stranger to my childhood.

AUNT JEANNE'S LEGACY

When Shanna was a little girl, she loved her Aunt Jeanne. They would spend quality time together and especially enjoyed shopping, taste testing all 27 flavors at the local ice cream parlor or going to the county fair. Aunt Jeanne taught Shanna how to appreciate beautiful flower gardens and how to weed and care for the summer vegetable garden. Shanna would giggle as she sprinkled the seedlings with warm water from the silver-colored watering can, pretending to give them a bath. Aunt Jeanne and Shanna would talk to the little seedlings and encourage them to sprout and grow upright and strong.

Without Shanna realizing it, Aunt Jeanne was speaking encouragement and strength into her young life, too.

Aunt Jeanne wasn't married. She had been engaged to an aviator who was missing in action during WWII; and apparently she never fell in love again. Instead, she filled her life with service to others: her parents until their deaths; her Sunday school children; her accounting job until she retired; and her women's sewing circle. Her heart's desire had been to teach kindergarten, but her father would not permit her to attend college. It wasn't a money issue, rather a cultural issue. Aunt Jeanne submitted to her father's authority.

During Shanna's teen years, she became obsessed with the physical appearance of things. Her clothes, hair, make-up, and her carefully selected friends–everything had to be perfect. Shanna didn't like people who were chubby or unattractive. She was athletic and popular, and couldn't understand why anyone wouldn't want to be just like her.

As Aunt Jeanne grew older, her physical appearance changed. She gained weight, developed arthritis and became sedentary. Additional hormonal changes caused several dark moustache hairs to sprout around her upper lip.

Shanna's teen friends would twitter and giggle about it, and dubbed them "mouse whiskers." When Aunt Jeanne would ask why they were being so silly, they'd cover their mouths and explode with laughter, excluding her from their cruel joke.

Shanna moved away from her hometown after she graduated from college —and seldom told Aunt Jeanne when she returned for visits. Through the years Shanna would send birthday greetings and Christmas cards and call Aunt Jeanne on the phone; but didn't want to be seen with a non-perfect person.

When Shanna was about 40 years old, she received a phone call from a former neighbor advising her that Aunt Jeanne had become critically ill. Shanna was contacted as her last surviving relative.

The five hour drive to her hometown gave Shanna an opportunity to reminisce about Aunt Jeanne's life.

She remembered the love and care Aunt Jeanne showed her when she was a little girl; and anguished over her own snobbish attitude as a teen.

Aunt Jeanne recognized Shanna when she walked into her room at the nursing home and attempted to hug her. But Shanna used the presence of intravenous tubes, oxygen, and monitors surrounding her as an excuse to avoid physical contact. Shanna hated hospitals almost as much as she hated imperfect people.

It was apparent that Aunt Jeanne was in physical distress and had become quite frail. They talked for only a few minutes before Aunt Jeanne drifted off into a drug-induced sleep. Shanna decided to pick up a few items from Aunt Jeanne's house and return to the nursing home later in the evening.

Aunt Jeanne's modest house was tastefully decorated just as Shanna remembered. The living room containing her TV, couch, reading chairs and piano hadn't changed throughout the years. "She always had nice things and took good care of them," Shanna mused.

Shanna walked up the thickly-carpeted stairs to the second floor, smiling as she remembered how as a little girl, she used to slide down the stairs on a piece of cardboard. There was always that one step half-way up that creaked…yes. It was still there.

Aunt Jeanne's hope chest was positioned on the landing, where it had always been. Young girls of her era would begin putting away items they'd need for marriage. It was a rite-of-passage in her society. Shanna hesitated before peeking inside—as if she was trespassing into Aunt Jeanne's very soul. The hope chest contained items of antiquity: hand stitched aprons, crochet doilies; and items she had never expected: taffeta formal gowns in radiant colors, a bridal dress and veil, and photos of Aunt Jeanne and her fiancé when they were newly engaged. She was lovely and slim, just as Shanna had been at her age. She also found Sunday school rosters with the names of dozens of children who had attended Aunt Jeanne's classes. How many children she had encouraged and inspired? How many Bible stories had she read and scripture verses had she made the children commit to memory?

Shanna had attended Aunt Jeanne's Sunday school classes as a child, but didn't continue going to church as a teen. She viewed religion as a crutch for feeble-minded people.

Shanna gathered Aunt Jeanne's nightgown, bathrobe and a few toiletries and returned to the nursing home. The nurses told her that several friends had visited and Aunt Jeanne was exhausted. "She needs some quiet and rest," they explained.

Shanna intended to sit beside Aunt Jeanne for an hour, and then return to her house to begin planning the funeral, and disposition of Aunt Jeanne's possessions. However, Shanna dozed off and awoke about 2:00 a.m., momentarily confused by her surroundings. Aunt Jeanne was gazing at her, almost as if she had been waiting for Shanna to open her eyes.

"Don't be startled, dear. I've been lying here quietly praying for you while you slept," she said.

Shanna looked surprised, but was warmed by Aunt Jeanne's concern.

"I've know you all your life, and you're as pretty now as when you were a little girl." Aunt Jeanne struggled to form her words, then continued, "You know, Shanna, people are impressed by outward appearances—how we look, what we do for a living and where we live; but God looks at the heart of a person."

She extended her hand and grasped Shanna's perfectly manicured fingers.

She continued, "You were always such a delight to be near and I cherished our visits. I've been remembering how we planted and tended our gardens together; and our fun adventures. It was a joy watching you grow up into a fine young lady." There were pauses between the sentences as Aunt Jeanne struggled for breath; but she seemed to be determined to continue speaking.

She looked directly into Shanna's brown eyes and asked, "What's going to happen to me?"

Shanna stammered and hesitatingly answered, "I...I don't know Aunt Jeanne. I hope the doctors and nurses help you...."

Aunt Jeanne squeezed Shanna's hand. She had asked the question to discern what Shanna believed.

"No, Shanna. I am beyond their help. There is only One who can help me now, and I've trusted Him to help me all my life. He could be your helper, too, if you let Him."

"Do you remember when you were a little girl and I told you about Jesus? He is the only perfect person who ever lived on earth, yet He allowed himself to become imperfect by taking our sin upon himself. This was necessary so we could be spiritually reunited with God, our heavenly Father, who is also perfect. I'd like to show you how you can have Jesus as your helper now; and be with me in eternity."

Tears streamed down Shanna's cheeks causing her perfectly applied makeup to smear, as Aunt Jeanne led her in a simple prayer. As she held tightly to Aunt Jeanne's hand, she asked God to forgive her for being prideful and arrogant; and for other attitudes and behaviors that were not pleasing to Him.

She sobbed as she invited Jesus into her life, and asked Him to help her become a woman seeking after His own heart.

In a few minutes, Shanna regained her composure and wiped her eyes; then realized that Aunt Jeanne's hand was no longer gripping onto hers. As she leaned over to kiss Aunt Jeanne one last time, the notorious mouse whiskers brushed against her cheek. "Thank you for understanding and forgiving me, Aunt Jeanne—just as Jesus understands and forgives us," she whispered.

When Shanna told the nurses what had happened, she was surprised by their response. "We knew your Aunt Jeanne wanted to talk with you tonight. Her chart shows that she refused her sleep medications so she could be awake and coherent. The duty nurse tried to contact you but when she couldn't reach you, she contacted the doctor. It was obvious that she had something important to say. Was she able to do that?"

Shanna responded without hesitation, "She shared something of eternal importance, and I'd like to share it with you…"

A smile of acknowledgement passed between the two nurses. As one nurse placed a comforting arm around Shanna's shoulders she explained: "Shanna, we think we know what you want to share with us. You see, Nurse Carol and I are sisters. We were in Aunt Jeanne's Sunday school class with you years ago. When Aunt Jeanne came into the nursing home, we recognized her name and have been praying with her every day. She also asked us to pray for you.

She loves you like a daughter and wants you to be with her in heaven."

Shanna hugged the two nurses as years of selfishness and pride dissolved in tears of joy. "I will be," she assured them.

"We know this is a difficult time for you but Aunt Jeanne would want you to be content. She asked us to tell you something else when this happened," said Carol. She asked us to tell you, "Welcome to the family!"

VALUABLE LESSONS

I once learned a valuable lesson through the actions of a puppy we were raising. I had put the older dogs outside in the kennel, but kept this young puppy in the house for his protection and training. He was contentedly stretched out on the "dog couch" – fully aware that he was momentarily occupying the place reserved for the Alpha dog. He kept a watchful eye on me as I worked in the kitchen and occasionally would raise his head in response to an unfamiliar noise or a tantalizing smell.

As I prepared dinner, I tucked aside a few choice morsels of stir fried chicken; then called the puppy into the kitchen to reward him. To my astonishment, the puppy refused to leave the luxury of the dog couch and instead whined and barked from his perceived place of honor on the couch.

I dangled the chicken in front of him and watched his eyes light up with delight and his tail respond with continuous wags of joy…but he would not leave the couch to claim his reward.

"Ok, puppy" I exclaimed. If you want this treat, you have to come to me."

Still he refused to leave the security and familiarity of the couch.

"Well, foolish little puppy, if you won't make the effort to walk to the kitchen, I'll give this choice morsel to another dog," I cajoled.

Still no response. I could have picked up the puppy and carried him into the kitchen, but he would not have learned an important lesson about obedience, trust and reward.

Often, when God has a particularly important lesson for us to learn, He presents it to us in several different formats. Later that evening, I heard an internationally-known evangelist discussing this same topic.

It seems many years ago when he was starting his ministry, he was a featured speaker at an outdoor camp meeting which lasted five days. The camp meeting was being held in the middle of a field where there were no restaurants, except for a chili wagon; so he stopped at a restaurant to eat before going to the camp meeting. The only money he had was a $50.00 bill which he used to pay for his breakfast. He was about to leave the restaurant when God spoke to him to give a certain man in the restaurant all the money he had received as change from his breakfast. Of course, he questioned whether he truly heard from God; and argued with himself that if he gave his money away, he wouldn't be able to buy food for the rest of the week. The young evangelist decided to be obedient and give the unknown man all his money.

At the close of the day, hungry and exhausted from preaching several hours, the young evangelist went to the tent where the preachers and musicians could rest. To his surprise, there was a hot dinner and cold beverage waiting for him. No one seemed to know who brought the food; and it was not supplied for anyone else. This continued every day of the camp meeting.

Years later, now a well-known international evangelist, he was greeting people after holding a revival. An elderly woman approached him and asked if he enjoyed the home-cooked meals she brought him during his camp meeting years ago. He asked the woman why she did that; and she responded that she was instructed by God to cook him dinner every night of the camp meeting!

This was an "Ah-ha!" moment for me. God spoke to my heart about how my actions either confirm or challenge my obedience and trust in Him. How many times had God attempted to bless me, but I missed the reward because I refused to leave my place of comfort or believe He was speaking to me? The poignant life lessons hit the mark!

More than ever, we need to put our trust in God and cultivate a closer relationship with Him. When we daily read His Word—pray and praise Him —seek His direction when making decisions—and are obedient when He instructs us to do something, He promises eternal rewards far beyond anything we can imagine.

He is calling to you right now and encouraging you, as He makes a way for you in the desert: "Arise, my love."

www.ingramcontent.com/pod-product-compliance
Lightning Source LLC
Chambersburg PA
CBHW061716120626
46550CB00003B/1253